About the Authors

Born and raised in Montreal, Camilia and Victoria are self-proclaimed veterans of karma. Having suffered enough trials and tribulations as payment for the reckless stunts they pulled as mindless young adults, they have accumulated enough suffering to land themselves a minor role in a religious text.

"As experts in Karma, we feel qualified to share our first-world wisdom, karma's a bitch and we learned it firsthand," says Camilia.

"Oh yeah! We were rough," agrees Victoria.

Pick up a copy today! If you don't, I'm sure you'll come around... most things do.

Pass It On (For Good Karma)

Written By Camilia Raven
Illustrated by Victoria Le Piane

Pass It On (For Good Karma)

Vanguard Press

VANGUARD PAPERBACK

© Copyright 2021
Camilia Raven
Illustrated by Victoria Le Piane

The right of Camilia Raven to be identified as author of
this work has been asserted by her in accordance with the
Copyright, Designs and Patents Act 1988.

All Rights Reserved

No reproduction, copy or transmission of this publication
may be made without written permission.
No paragraph of this publication may be reproduced,
copied or transmitted save with the written permission of the publisher, or in accordance with the provisions
of the Copyright Act 1956 (as amended).

Any person who commits any unauthorised act in relation to
this publication may be liable to criminal
prosecution and civil claims for damages.

A CIP catalogue record for this title is
available from the British Library.

ISBN 9781784659431

Vanguard Press is an imprint of
Pegasus Elliot MacKenzie Publishers Ltd.

www.pegasuspublishers.com

First Published in 2021

Vanguard Press
Sheraton House Castle Park
Cambridge England

Printed & Bound in Great Britain

Dedication

We'd like to dedicate this number to the Universe;
we hope this earns us brownie points somehow.

Acknowledgements

We would both like to wholeheartedly thank our amazing parents for their love, support, and money.

You Will Never Be Able To Unread The Following Page

A little exercise in motivated encoding:

What if we thought about karma the same way we would a slinky? Can you imagine it?

Let me paint you a picture:

So, there's this coil, olive green in colour

and metallic in texture (probably aluminum). These details

are irrelevant to the point, but relevant to the crafting of this picture.

Now envision me taking hold of this slinky by its two ends and pulling them out,

until the slinky resembled an epic waterslide.

Now, let us sit a child

down in front of our

vertically-stretched

slinky, so that

they have a

limited view

beyond the surface they're facing.

I'll then pierce a bead at the top of the slinky wire

and let go, so it'll slowly make its way down the slinky.

All the child will see is the bead coming in from the right side, sliding across,

and disappearing around the left side. After a few rotations, the kid will have pieced together that what goes around, must come around. In conclusion, that's what karma is.

Except not at all.

That was just a longwinded metaphor

for the common idiom, "What goes around, comes around".

You're welcome.

Now, you're probably pretty annoyed

and pondering ways to get even with me for shamelessly

wasting your time like that, I'm sure

an important big shot like yourself probably has a ton going on.

So, what'll it be? Perhaps,

tossing this book out the window? No, no, that won't matter, you already bought it.

That'll just be a you-problem.

Don't make yourself sick trying to get even, just acknowledge your grievances,

forgive me, and trust that the universe

will find its own sick way to make me miserable in due time.

And THAT'S karma. Bam. You've been universed.

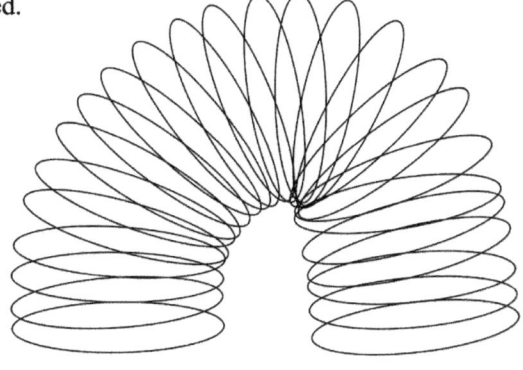

On Break! Be Back in 10… days.

The soft-edged beauty of indefinable accents
provides solace in presence, rather than absence.
Accept your hiatus and stop seeking a saviour.
Intermittent stasis doesn't make you a failure.

Try hard at hard times, but don't work yourself dead.
Some days, your accomplishment is staying in bed.
When time is frozen, we become very small
Because silence is golden and quiet is calm.

Act IV, Scene I.

Ashes to ashes
Dust to dust
Love was never built on lust
Up to the heavens
Down to the ground
What once was lost can surely be found
Ripening fruits all fated to spoil
United we stand, by trouble and toil.

Self-Care

Lavender baths and pumpkin lip butter.
Learn to let go of emotional clutter.
Cinnamon rose candles—so therapeutic.
And music.
There's always music.

Scarlett Fever

No gleam could enhance her.
No sheen could redeem her.
Her own brand of cancer,
The cynical dreamer.

Karmic Law

It goes around, circling the drain.
Unrecognizable, by face or by name.
Karmic in nature, the old ball and chain.
The universe's currency.
Lose what you gain.

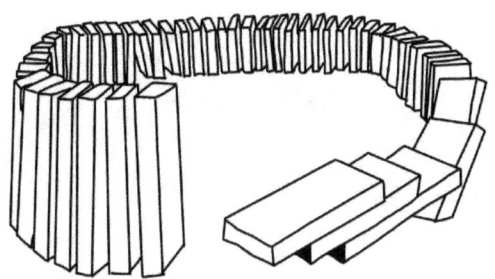

What We Deserve

Apologize. Acquit.
Own up to your shit.
Swallow your pride.
Repent and admit.
Surrender control
Or you'll end up alone.
It's one hell of a ride
And karma's a bitch.

Edges

There are two kinds of pain:
One makes me come and
one makes me leave.
I've no interest nor shame
to be candid nor vain
Or to spend my best days
with a heart on my sleeve.

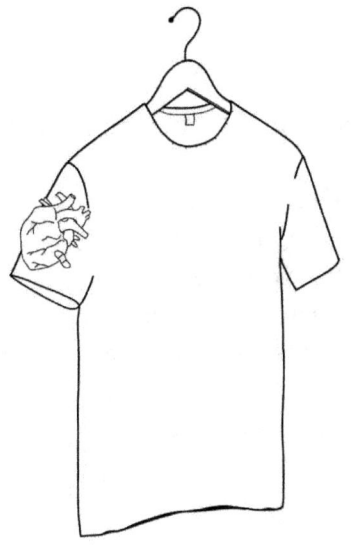

In Memory of the Time You Wasted—

I think that I got over you.
It took about a day or two.
PSYCH! It took an afternoon
Of sipping wine and humming tunes,
Of moving on and dodging ruin.
Eventually I survived somehow,
I'm finally sleeping soundly now.

Limerick on Perspective–

There once was a bitch named Mel,
Who never wished anyone well;
She gossiped and glared
to find someone who cared;
her mind was her personal hell.

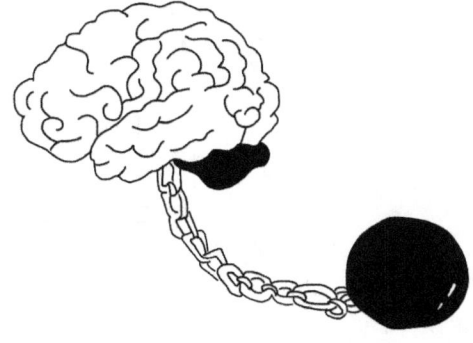

April 15th, 2019
17,946 steps - Running from problems

Some people won't like you, just say it's their loss.
Their personal view of how you come across.

Maybe how you are, they say you're a lot,
Either talking too much or lost in a thought.
Like we fell out of touch, but we never forgot.
We were hooked on a rush, loath to get caught.

There's no need to explain after every mistake.
Try solving some problems by walking away.

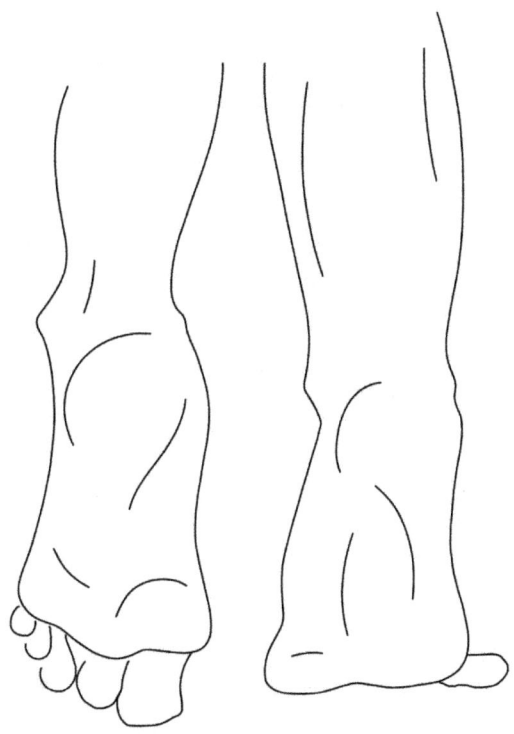

Hostile Work Environment

Opinions.
Volumes on volumes
That nobody need ever read.
No treasure to be preserved.
Every morning, slow and un-caffeinated.
Every night, wired and rushed.
I wait for her to leave.
So perhaps, at last,
I can once again—
Breathe.

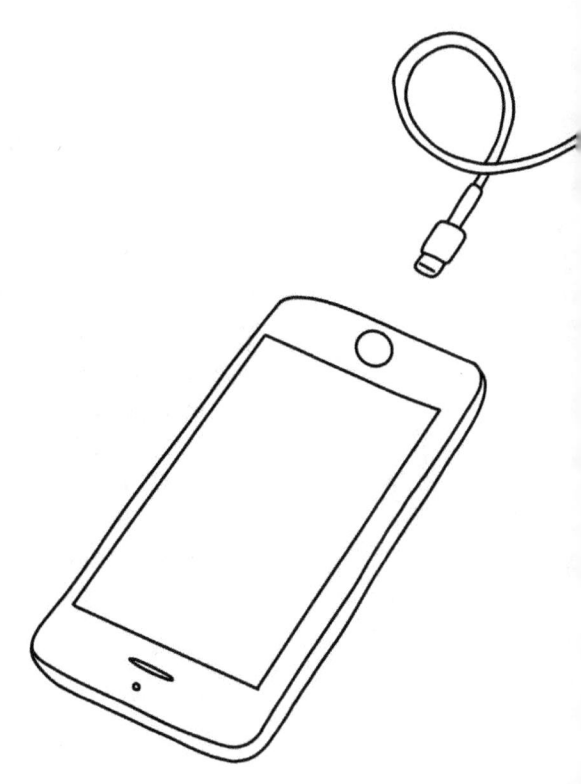

"Siri, can you please Google 'Idioms about Karma'?"

Thou shalt not covet— nor speak of it.
Reversal of fortune—you rise above it.
Sealing your fate—before you can start.
Merry ye meet and merry ye part.
A series of holding on and letting go.
Remembering ever, you reap what you sow.
Sometimes you fail—
And sometimes you grow—
Unity bound;
As above, so below.

deadplantsmom

The First Principle

There's a dualistic cosmology that philosophizes balance, in which I am myself with my own distinct talents and you're either faithful or drowned by your malice but opposing forces can reinstate status for light to protect while darkness wreaks havoc.

Wilted Wards and Hilt-less Swords

No rest for the wicked, break their spell.
Heal your wounds, be treated well.
Shield your fragile heart from harm,
Cherish all with humble charm.
Take care to think before you speak,
We find our strength when we are weak.
Refuse what you won't settle for.
Quoth the wilted: "Nevermore".

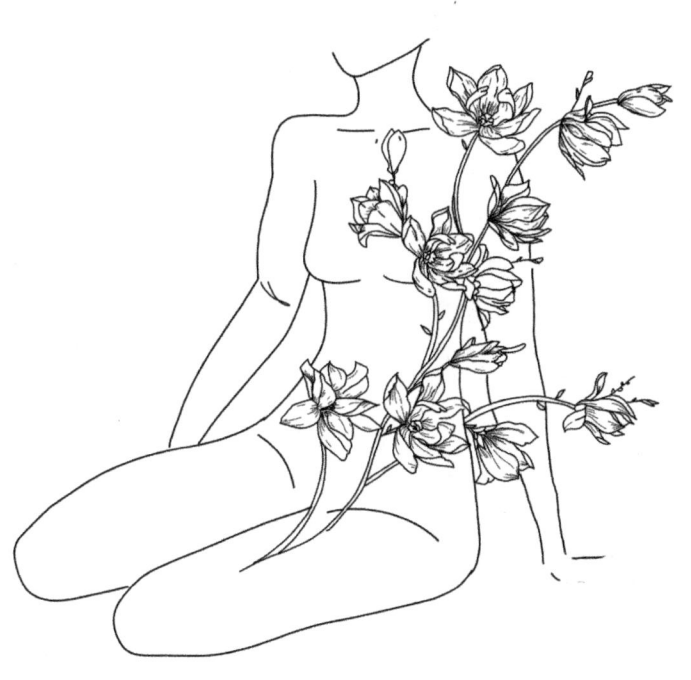

Forgiveness means 'Life Goes On'

Do it for laughter. Do it for passion.
Live for adventure. Never grow passive.
Life's smallest pleasures are also its magic.
Blaze a new trail. Don't follow the fashions.
Mindfully, you can live through your actions.
Slightly ambitious, but there's no harm in asking.
Days of distractions, dreams get abandoned,
regrets come flashing, they're closing your casket.
Who would have fathomed,
that we couldn't get past it?

Broken-hearted Martyrs, Pay Attention:

Reject the war between damnation and ascension.
Better hurt in the past than destroyed in the present.
Let mistakes be your lesson.
Let your pain be your blessing.
Don't strain to impress them.
Or spend days asking questions,
finding ways to address them,
To conflate or depress them,
though you'll never quite guess them.

I guess being vain is their test, then.

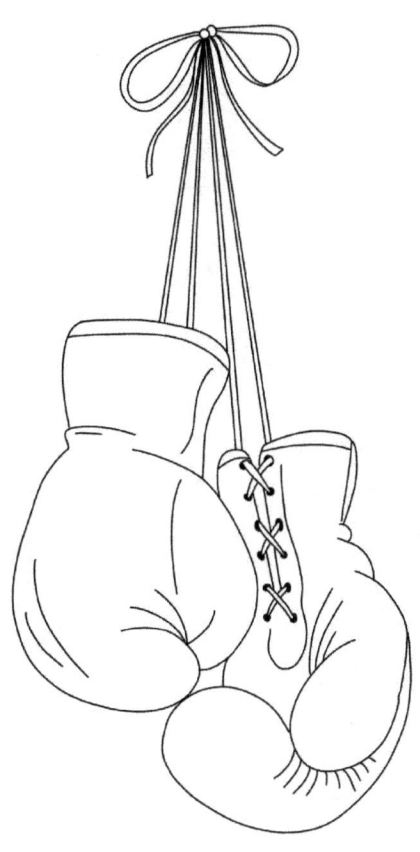

Who Cares?

I told her she made things better,
she replied with, "Whatever."
I said love made me a fool,
and she muttered, "That's cool."
I called her witty, smart, and pretty
and she told me she was busy.

Her eyes, always rolling.
Her life, never fair.
There's nothing quite as scary
As someone who doesn't care.

Well-Wishers at the Wishing Well

I spend most of my days counting.
Time. Weight. Money. Surrounded
by numbers that keep me grounded,
until I end up at a fountain
with a wish and a bag of change.
My reflection looks deranged,
My reflection is my stage.
I pour in my bag of treasure,
"Man, I wish things would get better."

"Keep Your Arms And Legs Inside The Vehicle For the Duration Of This Ride"

Don't trade your naivety with so much haste.
Soon, your first moments will be replaced
with the waves of the wind and the bitter taste
of a colder and slightly sharper place.

Avoid being wary or needlessly cruel.
Remember to pause,
breathe,
rest,
and refuel.
Your lifetime is a series of opening doors,
The choices you make will always be yours.

Move Along, Mind the Gap

They say it's better to say nothing than be caught in a lie,
And it's stronger to break down than it is not to cry,
And it's harder to see than to turn a blind eye.
Experience can't lighten the weight of goodbye.

The heart grows not fonder nor calmer at ease
by distance; we ponder who answers our pleas.
Who'd listen to wishes as desperate as these?
Shouted up to the heavens and lost in a breeze?

We can only move forward, we can never undo,
But you can only move forward if you do it for you.

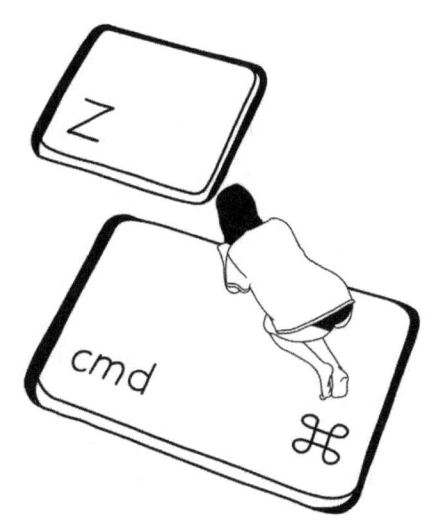

Mephisto's Contract

Winning comes at a heavy cost, for none is won if none is lost.
And if one falls for you to rise, then you grow rich as he grows wise.

They tell you not that love can see. It's only blind if we agree
to take each other at our word as resting eyes that rest assured.

Love is patient, love is kind, but somehow leaves us all behind
to deal with negative effects and glumly wonder what comes next.

Though we who ponder come to find: before contract was even signed,
That Faustus aged and lost his mind to the fatal flaw of humankind.

Power is no gift to give and time's a foe we can't outlive.
Be not wasted settling scores, all beginnings need closing doors.

Closure is not given, it is taken.

Despite all the suffering or parts you enjoyed,
Nothing but time will replenish the void.
Though already, it seems to be passing too slow;
Grass will not green if you're watching it grow.
It appears we did nothing but watch our love fail
or fight until arguments grew dull and stale.
I know only now that we held hands through hell
and as much as it pains me, I do wish you well.

lol k bye

An Open Letter to all my haters;
What goes around comes around.

YOU HEAR THAT, GUYS? SOMETHING BIG'S COMING
YOUR WAY (DE FACTO) THE UNIVERSE. DON'T BOTHER
RUNNING OR HIDING, THE UNIVERSE IS OBVIOUSLY
BEYOND YOUR LEVEL OF ATHLETICISM AND STEALTH.
SO, BEFORE YOU GO OFF WREAKING YOUR HAVOC,
JUST REMEMBER THAT A LARGE ENERGY-FORCE BITCHSLAP
IS DESTINED TO COME YOUR WAY, IF YOU DO.

Sincerely,
Ya Girls,
Overthinky and The Brain

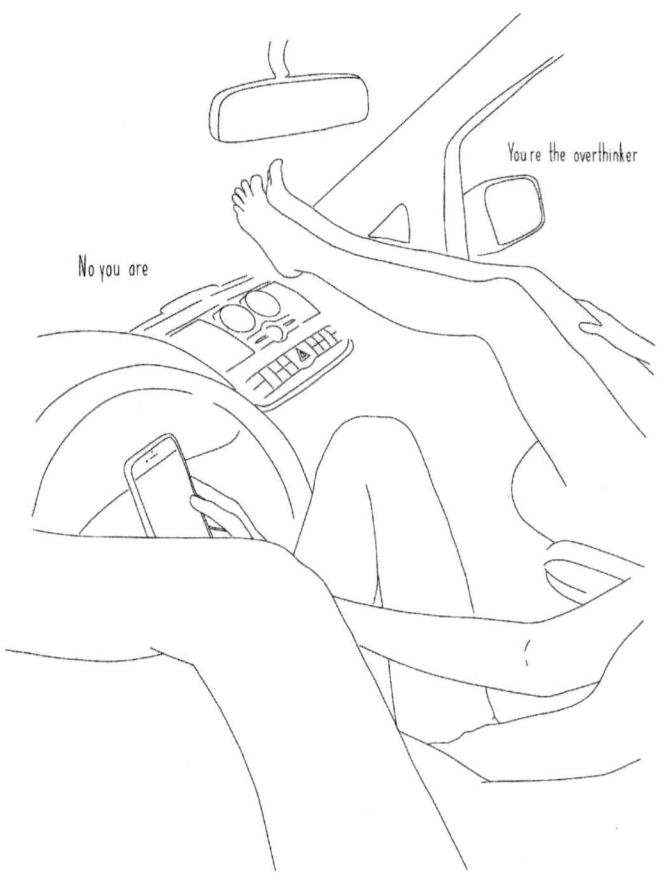

Fin.

www.ingramcontent.com/pod-product-compliance
Lightning Source LLC
LaVergne TN
LVHW081525060526
838200LV00044B/2003